The Eleventh Chester Book of Motets
The Flemish and German Schools for 5 voices

Edited by Anthony G. Petti

LIST OF MOTETS

T0052898

CHESTER MUSIC

AVE MARIA

Hail Mary, full of grace, the Lord is with you, blessed are you among women, alleluia.

Clemens non Papa (c. 1500-56)

CH55261

5

JUSTORUM ANIMAE

The souls of the just are in the hands of God, and the torment of death shall not touch them: in the sight of the unwise they seem to die, but they are at peace. (*Wisdom*, 3, i-iii)

Orlandus Lassus (c.1532–1594)

* Bars 27-33, black notation all parts without a preliminary time signature.

PECCANTEM ME QUOTIDIE

The fear of death terrifies me, for I sin daily without repenting. Have pity on me, at least you, my friends, because the hand of God has struck me. Why do you pursue me as if you were God and sate yourselves with my flesh?(*Job,* 19, xxi-xxii)

Philipp de Monte(1521-1603)

STETIT JESUS

Jesus stood in the midst of his disciples and said: peace be with you, it is I, be not afraid, alleluia.
(*Luke*, 24, xxxvi)

Jacob Regnart (c. 1540-99)

JUBILATE DEO

Let all the world rejoice in God: serve the Lord with gladness; enter his presence with joy. Know that the Lord
is God: he made us and not we ourselves. (*Ps. 100,* i–iii)

Cipriano de Rore (1516–65)

MAGI VIDENTES STELLAM

The Magi, seeing the star, said to one another: "This is the sign of a great king. Let us go and seek him out and offer him gifts of gold, frankincense and myrrh, alleluia."

Blasius Amon (1560-90)

* Bars 63 iii-64 ii, alto and bass have been interchanged. + ♩ ♪ (G G F) in the original.

IN NOMINE JESU

At the name of Jesus let every knee bow in heaven, on earth and beneath the earth; and let every tongue proclaim that Jesus Christ the Lord lives in the glory of God the Father. (*Phil. 2,* x-xi)

Jacob Handl (1550-1591)

CANTATE DOMINO

Sing a new song to the Lord, let the whole earth sing to God. Sing to the Lord and bless his name: proclaim his salvation from day to day. Declare his glory among nations, his wonders among all peoples. For the Lord is powerful and greatly to be praised. He is awesome beyond all gods. (*Ps. 96,* i–iv)

Hans Leo Hassler (1564–1612)

ERIPE ME DE INIMICIS

Rescue me from my enemies, O Lord, when I fly to you. Teach me to do your will, for you are my God.
(*Ps. 143* , ix-x)

Andreas Raselius (c.1562-1602)

EDITOR'S NOTES

The aim of this present series is to make more readily available a comprehensive body of Latin motets from the Renaissance and Early Baroque periods, combining the inclusion of old favourites with the provision of lesser known or hitherto unpublished works. Generally speaking, all the pieces are within the scope of the reasonably able choir. They also encompass a fair selection from the liturgical year as a guide for use both in church and in the concert hall when performing choirs wish to present their programme according to theme or a particular season.

The editor has endeavoured to preserve a balance between a critical and performing edition. The motets are, where necessary, transposed into the most practical performing keys, are barred, fully underlayed, and provided with breathing marks. They also have a reduction either as a rehearsal aid or as a form of accompaniment, since at least some of the works of the later period were clearly intended to be reinforced by a continuo. Editorial tempi and dynamics are supplied only in the reduction, leaving choirmasters free to supply their own in the light of their interpretation of a given piece, vocal resources and the acoustics. The vocal range is given at the beginning of each motet. Also provided is a translation of every text and a table of use.

As an aid to musicologists, the motets are transcribed, wherever possible, from the most authoritative sources, and the original clefs, signatures and note values are given at the beginning and wherever they change during the course of a piece. Ligatures are indicated by slurs, editorial accidentals are placed above the stave, and the underlay is shown in italics when it expands a ditto sign, or in square brackets if editorial. Where the original contains a *basso continuo*, it is included as the bass line of the reduction. Figurings are not included, however, because they are usually extremely sparse, and do not normally indicate any more than the harmony already provided by the vocal parts. Finally, each volume includes a brief introduction concerning the scope of the edition, with notes on the composers, the motets, and the sources, together with a list of editorial emendations and alterations, if any.

This volume contains nine motets from the 16th and 17th centuries: the first five by Flemish composers, and the remaining four by German. The term German is interpreted loosely in order to include Austrian and Slovene composers. As with all of the volumes from nine to twelve in this series, the fifth voice is for soprano (occasionally mezzo soprano or alto), because this combination is probably the easiest for the average choir to accommodate.

Five-part motets are not especially numerous in the first part of the 16th century, but are prevalent towards the end, possibly as part of the trend towards polychoral writing. The fifth voice (often called Quintus or Quinta Vox) is generally drawn from the lower parts. However, as if in imitation of the madrigal style, the habit of using as the fifth voice a second cantus equal with the cantus one gradually comes into fashion by the final decades of the century.

Flemish composers were extremely influential in the late 15th and 16th centuries, and occupied key musical positions in many of the courts and major cathedrals of Europe. Italy was especially receptive to Flemings, who in turn became somewhat Italianised or Italianate, even to the point where some of them are best known by the Italian form of their names, including, in this volume, Orlando di Lasso and Cipriano de Rore.

The first composer, Jacobus Clemens non Papa (c.1500-c.1566-8), spent more of his life in his native country than did most of his fellow musicians of equivalent stature, though it can be inferred that he spent his early years in Paris. In later life he seems to have resided mainly in Ypres, acquiring the suffix "non Papa" to distinguish him from a fellow townsman, a poet called Jacobus Papa. (It should be noted that the theory that he acquired the title, whimsically or otherwise, to distinguish him from Pope Clement VII is now almost entirely discredited.) Clemens' sacred compositions are not only copious but also very inventive and of a uniformly high standard. In particular, he was a prolific composer of motets, of which eighty-eight are for five voices.

The five-part *Ave Maria* was not published in his lifetime, surviving in the Gemeentelijke Archiefdienst, Leyden, Choirbook E, ff. 65v.-6, in which it was ascribed at different times to "Gheerkin" and "Tho. Criquillon," though the present attribution has prevailed. The *Ave Maria* in some form or other was one of the most popular Marian texts, and many of the settings were based in varing degrees of closeness on the plainsong equivalent. Clemens' setting is no exception, for it begins with the plainsong intonation from one of the pre-Tridentine variants and then proceeds with a free paraphrase in imitation in the four upper parts, the Bass providing a loose inversion or moving independently. This pattern continues until the alleluia, with the Soprano I repeating in some form or other the plainchant alleluia four times. Though short, the motet is divided into three sections, as if each phrase was to take the full weight of meditation, a technique similar to that later used, for example, by Cornelius Verdonck in his *Ave gratia plena* (volume 6 of this series). While the work has not the usual mellifluousness of Clemens, it has an unobvious beauty and a quiet asceticism, reinforced by the subtle use of Hypoaeolian mode and final Phrygian cadence.

Orlandus Lassus (c.1532-94) is known by various forms of his name, including the Italian and Flemish versions, Orlando di Lasso and Rolande de Lattre. He probably began as a choirboy in his birthplace, Mons. Melodramatically, he was kidnapped on account of his beautiful voice and spirited off to Italy, where he soon entered the service of Ferdinand Gonzaga, and travelled widely, visiting Palermo, Naples and Milan. At twenty one he became choirmaster at St. John Lateran in Rome, but held the post only two years, returning to the Low Countries. After periods of travel in northern Europe, he was employed by the Duke of Bavaria in 1556. and remained attached to the Bavarian court for the rest of his life, though he was a frequent honoured guest in many capitals of Europe.

An extremely prolific composer, with well over 1,200 works to his credit (including five hundred motets), Lassus displays an extraordinary mastery of all forms and styles of vocal music current in his day. It is hard to believe, for example, that the extrovert and ribald madrigal, *Matona mia cara*, the delicate French love song, *Mon coeur se recommande à vous,* and the highly chromatic and etherial *Prophetiae sibyllarum*, each masterpieces in their own genre, all stem from the same pen. There are, however, a few places where Lassus appears to nod, or where the polyphony is a little dense. Some of his shorter masses are too utilitarian and brief, paying little attention to the syllabication or nuances of the words; and some of his motets are a little remote or too austere. But these observations are subjective, and scarcely can detract from the universal admiration which then, as now, caused him to be considered the greatest of the Renaissance Flemings.

The Lassus *Justorum animae* was first published in *Sacrae cantiones quinque vocum*, printed by Adam Berg in 1582 (transcribed from the complete set of part books in the British Library). It was also published, with minor variants in *Magnum opus musicum Orlandi di Lasso*, 1604. The work is remarkably tender and contains a masterly expression of faith in the afterlife. The optimism of the work is basically conveyed in the Ionian mode, though there is subtle alternation of major and minor until the work eventually comes to rest, steered home by the quiet, almost fauxbourdon passage alternating between subdominant, tonic and dominant ("sunt in pace"). The phrases are uniformly tender, though extremely expressive also, especially in the opening minor sixth leaps (Soprano I, bar 2, Alto, bars 2-3) and in the suspensions for "tormentum mortis," a very shapely descending phrase, especially in the two top parts. The motet has a remarkable degree of variety, and, despite its brief length, falls into at least four well-defined and often strongly contrasting sections, including a section in triple time for "insipientium mori." Further comments and a comparison with Byrd's masterly setting (also for the same vocal combination) are contained in volume nine of this series. It should be added that the text in Lassus' time, that is, before the revision of the missal by Clement VIII, read "mortis" for "malitiae", and did not include an alleluia.

Lassus is followed in this volume by his close friend, Philippe de Monte (1521-1603). Monte was born in Malines but spent much of his early life in the Spanish kingdom of Naples. He journeyed to England with Philip II of Spain during the first year of the king's marriage to Mary I, and probably made the acquaintance of William Byrd, then in his early teens, with whom he later conducted a musical correspondence. After spending some time in Antwerp, in 1568 he went to Vienna as maestro di cappella to the Emperor Maximilian II, upon whose death he was engaged by the next emperor, Rudolph II. He travelled with Rudolph to Prague, where he spent most of the rest of his life. De Monte's output is extremely large, and includes 30 volumes of madrigals and 34 masses. No four-part motets survive, however, accounting for his delayed appearance in this series.

Peccantem me quotidie is a searing penitential text, and attracted many fine settings, including those by Morales (see volume three), Palestrina, and Gesualdo, who lost no opportunity to exploit the unearthly chromaticism that the words encouraged. Monte's text, however, differs from the usual one by moving to *Job*, 19, xxi after the opening. The motet is a late work, and was published as no. 14 of *Sacrarum cantionum cum quinque vocibus . . . liber septimus*, Venice, Angelo Gardano, 1600 (copy in Bischöfliche Zentralbibliothek, Regensburg). The motet is remarkably restrained, even by comparison with Palestrina's setting. Dissonance is not particularly common, and is usually prepared, except for a notable clash between the Soprano II and the Tenor (bar 15), which would be clumsy were it not for the melodic considerations of the tenor line. Yet, while there is no chromaticism, leading notes are frequently raised, thereby lending something of an apocalyptic quality. There is, too, a restlessness of mode and key, even if, basically, the motet moves between the Aeolian and Phrygian, with strong hints of A Minor (transposed here to B Minor). Though its effects are not obvious, the motet has a remarkable power and sonority, and, as usually happens, appears more effective sung than it does on paper.

Jacob Regnart (c.1540-99) came from a musical family and three of his four brothers were also composers. Like Monte, whom he must have known, Jacob went into service at the courts in Vienna and Prague. He became a tenor in the imperial chapel in the 1560s, and in the 1570s became choirmaster and vice chapelmaster. During the last two decades of the 16th century he was in service with the Archduke Ferdinand at Innsbruck, though he spent the last five years of his life in Prague. Regnart published both secular music, which includes a series of German three-part lieder in Italian style, and sacred music, comprising mainly masses and motets.

The *Stetit Jesus* is no. 12 of *Sacrae aliquot cantiones quas moteta vulgus appellat, quinque et sex vocum*, Munich, Adam Berg, 1575 (complete set in the Staatsbibliothek der Stifting Preussicher Kulturbesitz, Berlin). A remarkably melodious and serene work which deserves to be far better known, it begins with a double fugue, one with an ornamented ascending passage in three parts, and another on a form of plainsong cantus firmus for the Soprano II and Alto. The work continues fugally (in contrast with the Peter Philips setting of *Surgens Jesus*, which is frequently chordal, e.g., "dixit: pax vobis") and frequently employs inversion or quasi inversion. Despite the fugal form, Regnart clearly preserves the outlines of each section, with minimal overlapping. Thus, the beautiful "pax vobis," with Soprano I and Tenor moving in tenths, is carefully prepared for. So also are the commanding "ego sum", where nearly all voices descend the triad, and the sprightly rhythmic section "nolite timere," where the Saviour seems to shake the apostles gently out of their petrifaction. The conclusion of the motet, an extended sequence of alleluias, is especially effective, its exuberant joy being expressed in fast runs and lively syncopation, so preventing the pervasive sweetness of the work from cloying.

Yet another Fleming with an Italianate name, Cipriano de Rore (1516-65), was born probably in Antwerp, where he trained as a choirboy. After his voice broke he went to Italy and became a pupil of a fellow Fleming, Adrian Willaert, maestro di cappella at St. Mark's, Venice. From 1547-58 he was in the service of the Duke of Ferrara, Ercole II, and shortly after became maestro di cappella to Ottavio Farnese, Duke of Parma. In 1562 he succeeded Willaert at St. Mark's, but quickly resigned the post to return to Parma. Rore has eight books of madrigals to his name, three volumes of motets, a Passion, and several masses.

The *Jubilate Deo* is part one of a double motet first published posthumously in *Cypriani de Rore sacrae cantiones . . . cum quinque sex et septem vocibus*, Venice 1595 (copy in Deutsches Musikgesichtliches Archiv, Kassel). While not as lively and forceful as most settings of this text (compare the Lassus setting in volume five of this series, but note the similar treatment of "servite"), it is very melodious, contains a wide variety of vocal textures, and has a certain amount of pace. It is set entirely fugally, with the voices rarely singing at once until towards the end, when a fine sense of climax is achieved. Each new subject flows easily and naturally from its predecessor. The polyphonic strands have a tunefulness akin to that of 19th century melody, though the cadential phrases are traditional, perhaps even a little trite. Rore also shows a fine regard for the shape of the verbal text, with pleasant though not especially original melismas for important words and syllables (e.g., "terra", "laetitia", "exsultatione".) The motet is mainly in the transposed Ionian mode, but eventually modulates unexpectedly into the Aeolian, and ends on a Phrygian cadence relative to that mode. Such a modulation is probably explicable in terms of the verbal text "et non ipsi nos."

The first of the Germanic composers in this volume, Blasius Amon or Ammon, lived only thirty years. He was born in Imst in the Tyrol in 1560, and died in Vienna in 1590. He began his musical career as a choirboy under the Archduke Ferdinand of Austria, who sent him to Venice to complete his musical studies. The influence of Venice is reflected in his being one of the first German composers, if not the first, to employ the double choir technique. In 1578, Amon joined the Franciscan order at Innsbruck, and then entered the Franciscan monastery in Vienna, where he became a priest. As might be expected, Amon's output is fairly small and includes no secular music. His work is, however, inventive and vigorous. *Magi videntes stellam* is no. 6 of a collection published in the year of his death, *Sacrae Cantiones* (copy in the Bischöfliche Zentralbibliothek, Regensburg). The motet has a sweeping and forceful movement and matches the wonderment and excitement of the words. Frequent use is made of sequential repetition; but various other stylistic effects are used as appropriate, including monosyllabic and melismatic treatment (cf. the extended runs on "eamus, inquiramus"), polyphony and homophony, duple and triple time. There is also a sense of antiphony, including the symbolic use of three voices (bars 31-9). The mode though superficially transposed Dorian, is mainly in Aeolian because of the raised E and flattened D (in this transposition), though it ends in the major. Summing up the features of the style is difficult, but the motet seems to be a skilful blend of Italian and Flemish features.

Jacob Handl (1550-91), sometimes known by the Latin form of his name, Jacobus Gallus, was born at Reifnitz, Carniola, but spent most of his life in Bohemia. He was a member of the Court chapel for a time, then chapelmaster to the Bishop of Olomouc, but from about 1568 spent the rest of his life in Prague. Handl's style varies considerably. He wrote large-scale works using double choirs in the Venetian manner, and intricate, harmonically sophisticated motets with abundant chromaticism; but he could also write entirely chordally in a simple and highly economical vein. The motet included here is closest to the last category described. No. 97 in *Quartus tomus musici operis, harmoniarum quatuor, quinque, sex, octo, et plurium vocum*, Prague, 1590 (copy in British Library), it is one of two settings which Handl made for the text, the first being a four-part version for lower voices published four years earlier in *Tomus primus musici operis*. The two settings have much in common. Both are mainly monophonic, fairly sustained in note values, sparing in the use of melisma, but have considerable modal variety. The resemblances between the two settings are especially noticeable in the opening phrases. Rhythmical similarity is striking throughout, even though the four-part setting moves into triple time for the last section beginning "in gloria est", while the five-part breaks into a short stretto fugue at this point. Again, the two pieces generally employ the same repetition of verbal phrases, with the main exception that whereas the earlier setting does not repeat "quia Dominus noster Jesus Christus," this phrase receives very prominent attention in the later version, being repeated four times. It should also be noted that a certain amount of word-painting appears in both, though more obviously in the five-part version. In particular, all voices have highlying, gently descending phrases for "caelestium", a middle-range, gently descending imitation for "terrestrium", and low-lying phrases for "infernorum", with a steep descent in the middle of the phrase in most voices. Although Handl has employed an extra voice in his second setting, much of it, nevertheless, is in four parts, there being usually an alternation between the tenor and the bass line, presumably to provide a contrast in tone; and when all five voices are used, it is generally for reinforcement, breadth, and to give a sense of climax.

Hans Leo Hassler (1564-1612) was born in Nuremberg of a very talented musical family. Early in life he went to study under Andrea Gabrieli in Venice and became a colleague of Giovanni Gabrieli. Returning to Germany, he obtained the post of organist to the Fuggers, and in 1602 was appointed hofkapellmeister in Nuremberg. He wrote a large number of sacred and secular works, and organ compositions. Like Handl, whom he resembles stylistically in many ways, Hassler uses a variety of techniques in his sacred compositions, some of them clearly derived from Giovanni Gabrieli, being especially evident in his polychoral compositions, and a few others taken from the Flemish composers. Though Hassler and Handl are similar, Hassler seems to be a much more extroverted and forthright composer, with a strong feeling for well-sustained and pleasing melodies, while Handl is rather more subtle and less flamboyant.

Hassler's *Cantate Domino* was first published as no. 27 of *Cantiones sacrae festis praecipuis totius anni, 4,5,6,7,8 & plurium vocum*, Augsburg, 1591 (copy in Bischöfliche Zentralbibliothek, Regensburg). It is one of three settings, the others being for four voices — the best known, published in volume four of this series — and for twelve voices. The four- and five-part settings have several features in common, especially in the "et benedicite nomini eius" section, where both use homophony in triple time and have a similar melodic line. They also have considerable rhythmic vitality. But whereas the four-part setting is mainly chordal and has an obvious immediate appeal, the five-part has a considerable amount of fugal and "mixed" passages, and is a little more subtle. Both are highly effective as expressions of openhearted joy and praise.

The last of the German composers, Andreas Raselius (c.1562-1602), was a Protestant, being the son of a Lutheran minister, though he nevertheless composed a great deal of Latin music appropriate for the Roman liturgy, as well as Lutheran chorales and vernacular motets. He was born in Heidelberg, studied at the University of Leipzig (1581-4) and was then appointed cantor at the Gymnasium in Regensburg. For the last two years of his life he was hofkapellmeister to the Elector Palatine, Frederick IV.

Raselius' *Eripe me de inimicis* survives in his manuscript anthology, *Dodecachordi vivi*, 1589 (no. 70 in MS AR. 774, Bischöfliche Zentralbibliothek, Regensburg). It is an austerely beautiful work which seems to be evocative of the penitential motets of Lassus and Handl. Especially delicate is the handling of the mode, whereby the Hypolydian moves to the Ionian, as the plea for help gives way to tranquil hope.

Editorial emendations

In nomine Jesu: Cantus, 17, i, A to A♭; Tenor, 45, iv, "De-" to "est"

Table of use according to the Tridentine Rite

Motet	Liturgical source	Seasonal or festal use
Ave Maria	Antiphon, Blessed Virgin; offertory, Immaculate Conception	Blessed Virgin
Justorum animae	Offertory, All Saints & Common of Martyrs	All Saints, feasts of martyrs
Peccantem me quotidie	7th responsory, Matins, Office of the Dead	All Souls, funerals, Lent
Stetit Jesus	Antiphon, Benedictus, Easter Tuesday	Easter
Jubilate Deo	Psalm, Lauds of Christmas	Christmas, general
Magi videntes stellam	Antiphon, Magnificat, 1st Vespers, Epiphany	Epiphany
In nomine Jesu	Antiphon and Introit, Holy Name	Holy Name, Christ
Cantate Domino	Psalm, Matins of Christmas	Christmas, general
Eripe me de inimicis	Psalm, Lauds, Good Friday; Compline, All Souls	Holy Week, All Souls, Lent